W9-CHZ-240

NASA

Salvatore Tocci

Franklin Watts
A Division of Scholastic Inc.
New York • Toronto • London • Auckland • Sydney
Mexico City • New Delhi • Hong Kong
Danbury, Connecticut

To all who have looked to the sky and asked "Why not?"

Note to readers: Definitions for words in **bold** can be found in the Glossary at the back of this book.

Photographs © 2003: AP/Wide World Photos/NASA: 45; Corbis Images: 51 (NASA), 7 (Stocktrek), 6; Finley-Holiday Films: 41; Mark Robinson: 39; NASA: 48 (Jet Propulsion Lab Photo), 47 (Marshall/GHCC), 36 (U.S. Geological Survey, Flagstaff, Arizona), cover, 3 left, 3 right, 4, 8, 11, 12, 14, 15, 17 bottom, 18, 20, 21, 22, 24, 25, 28, 30, 31, 33, 34, 42, 46, 50; Photo Researchers, NY: 40 (Mark Marten/NASA/SS); PhotoEdit/Michael Newman: 17 top.

Library of Congress Cataloging-in-Publication Data

Tocci, Salvatore.
     NASA / by Salvatore Tocci.
          p. cm. — (Watts library)
     Summary: Examines the function of NASA and discusses its various space exploration programs and achievements.
     Includes bibliographical references and index.
     ISBN 0-531-12282-4 (lib. bdg.)   0-531-15598-6 (pbk.)
     1. United States. National Aeronautics and Space Administration—History—Juvenile literature. 2. Astronautics—United States—History—Juvenile literature. [1. United States. National Aeronautics and Space Administration. 2. Astronautics.] I. Title. II. Series.
TL793.T63 2003
629.4'0973—dc21
                                                                              2003005818

Contents

NASA launched the world's first weather satellite in 1960. Seen here, the satellite was known as TIROS, which is an acronym for Television Infra-Red Observation Satellite.

Two Disasters

On September 8, 1900, a powerful hurricane raged through Galveston, Texas. Just before the hurricane struck the coastal town, winds were blowing at 135 miles (217 kilometers) per hour. As the hurricane passed through Galveston, it destroyed nearly three-quarters of the town. Between 8,000 and 10,000 people were killed. The hurricane that devastated Galveston was the deadliest natural disaster in U.S. history.

On August 24, 1992, the costliest natural disaster in U.S. history struck Florida. This was Hurricane Andrew. Packing winds as strong as those that had

The hurricane that destroyed the Texas port city of Galveston on September 8, 1900, claimed more than 8,000 lives, making it the most deadly storm in U.S. history.

struck Galveston, Andrew tore across southern Florida in just four hours. The storm blew apart nearly 80,000 buildings and left almost 200,000 people homeless. Hurricane Andrew caused a record $30 billion in damage. Amazingly, only twenty-six people were killed as a direct result of the storm, mostly from flying debris and collapsing buildings.

Why did a hurricane kill so many people in Texas in 1900, when a hurricane just as powerful killed so few in 1992? Part of the answer can be found in the sky where weather satellites **orbit** Earth. A **satellite** is any object that orbits another object in space. In 1992, images from a weather satellite revealed that a major hurricane was approaching Florida. As a result, people were advised to seek shelter before Hurricane Andrew struck.

Back in 1900, the people in Texas were not as fortunate. The National Aeronautics and Space Administration (NASA) did not launch the first weather satellite until 1960. Since then, these satellites have probably helped save thousands of lives. When you think of NASA, you probably picture astronauts flying aboard the space shuttle or an unmanned

The Birth of NASA

NASA was established on July 29, 1958, when President Dwight D. Eisenhower signed the bill passed by Congress to set up the space agency. NASA began operating on October 1, 1958.

spacecraft speeding toward a distant planet. Although NASA's mission is to explore and study the universe, all of us who have never left Earth have benefited from NASA's work. Weather satellites are only part of the story.

Today, weather satellites and other imaging technology can track the progress of potentially deadly storms. Seen here is a time-lapse photograph of Hurricane Andrew approaching the Florida coast and crossing into the Gulf of Mexico.

Together, the spacecraft, lunar module, and Saturn rocket that comprised Apollo 11 towered 363 feet (111 meters) above the launch pad at what was then known as the Kennedy Space Center in Florida. These vehicles would send astronauts Neil Armstrong, Edwin "Buzz" Aldrin, and Michael Collins to the Moon.

Chapter One

Humans in Space

What do the following items have in common: cordless power tool, television satellite dish, smoke detector, and water filter? You may have answered that all these items can be found in a home, perhaps even your own. All these items also have something else in common, however. They all use technologies or materials that were originally developed by NASA to send astronauts into space.

The First Astronauts

NASA was designed as a civilian organization in charge of the United States' exploration of space. One of its first goals was to send humans into space. In 1959, NASA chose seven military pilots to be its first astronauts, a word that means "sailors of the stars." These seven men became known as the Mercury 7. Mercury, the speedy messenger of the gods in Roman mythology, was the name NASA chose for its project to send its first astronauts into space.

America, however, would not be the first nation to send an astronaut into space. The **Soviet Union** launched a man named Yuri Gagarin into space on April 12, 1961. Gagarin orbited Earth once. His successful mission was a wake-up call for NASA to send an American astronaut into space.

On May 5, 1961, NASA launched its first astronaut, Alan Shepard, from Cape Canaveral, Florida. Although NASA's success followed the Soviet Union's by only twenty-three days, the two country's space flights were very different. Gagarin had circled Earth and reached a speed of 17,544 miles (28,228

Race to the Moon

Just twenty days after Shepard's flight, President John F. Kennedy addressed Congress and said, "I believe that this nation should commit itself to achieving the goal, before the decade is out, of landing a man on the Moon and returning him safely to Earth." There was no doubt—the United States and the Soviet Union were in a race to be the first country to send astronauts safely to the Moon and back. The race would last for over eight years.

km) per hour. In contrast, Shepard traveled just 303 miles (488 km) east of Cape Canaveral and reached a speed of only 5,134 miles (8,261 km) per hour. Unlike Gagarin, however, Shepard could control the movements of his spacecraft. He could make it move up and down, side to side, and roll.

NASA first sent an astronaut into orbit around Earth on February 20, 1962, ten months after Gagarin's flight. It had taken NASA that long to build a rocket powerful enough to send an American high enough into space to enter orbit. The astronaut, John Glenn, orbited Earth three times in a flight that lasted almost five hours.

Three more Mercury flights followed Glenn's. The last one left Earth on May 15, 1963. On that flight, the astronaut, Gordon Cooper, circled Earth twenty-two times in just over thirty-four hours. Cooper became the first astronaut to sleep in space. With the success of its Mercury project, NASA showed that humans could travel safely in space for an extended period of

time. Now it was time for NASA to move on to the next step in landing astronauts on the Moon.

Project Gemini

To go to the Moon and back, astronauts would have to travel as a team. They would also have to leave their spacecraft and perform an **extra-vehicular activity** (**EVA**), which is commonly called a space walk. Finally, a journey to the Moon would require two spacecraft to meet and dock in space. NASA designed Project Gemini to meet all these goals. The name of this project came from the Latin word for "twins." Each spacecraft in Project Gemini carried two astronauts.

Between March 1965 and November 1966, NASA

launched ten successful Gemini flights. During the second Gemini flight, Edward White became the first American to perform an EVA. The space suit that White wore had many features designed to protect him from the conditions in space. For example, the suit had to maintain his body temperature even though the temperature in space went from 250° Fahrenheit (121° Celsius) in the sun to -150° F (-101° C) in the shade.

The next Gemini flight set a record that lasted for five years. The two astronauts aboard the spacecraft orbited Earth for almost eight days. This flight proved that astronauts could live and work in space long enough to go to the Moon and back, a round-trip that would take eight days.

After five Gemini flights, NASA had proven that it could send two astronauts into space for long periods of time. NASA had also shown that astronauts could perform EVAs. All that remained was to have two spacecraft meet and dock in space. Docking would be required to land astronauts on the Moon. While a manned spacecraft continued to orbit the Moon, a small landing craft with astronauts aboard would be sent to the lunar surface. The landing craft would then lift off from the Moon and meet up and dock with the orbiting craft for the return trip to Earth.

The first Gemini flight to dock successfully was launched on March 16, 1966. Once in orbit, the two astronauts aboard started chasing an unmanned spacecraft that had been launched hours earlier from Cape Canaveral. The astronauts succeeded in catching and docking with the other spacecraft.

UFOs

Gordon Cooper was the first astronaut in space to report seeing unidentified flying objects (UFOs).

Earth. Although it was NASA's last manned mission to the Moon, this Apollo flight marked another first for America. One of the astronauts, Harrison Schmitt, became the first scientist to travel in space. While on the Moon, Schmitt set up several experiments. He also used the cordless power tools that NASA had developed to bring back about 245 pounds (111 kg) of lunar rocks and soil samples.

NASA Spinoffs

Cordless power tools are only one of the many products used in homes today that were first developed by NASA. Such products are known as **spinoffs**, items originally developed for one purpose that are redesigned or modified for another purpose. Perhaps you have never used a cordless power tool. But you probably have used other spinoffs from NASA's projects to send astronauts to the Moon.

For example, you may use a joystick to play games on your computer. NASA developed the first joystick so that astronauts could control the vehicle they used to roam the lunar surface. You may wear sunglasses that block almost all the sunlight that can damage your eyes. These glasses are a spinoff of a visor NASA developed to protect an astronaut's eyes from sunlight during an EVA. Even more spinoffs have come from the technology NASA developed to place space stations in orbit around Earth.

A boy uses a joystick to play a computer game. Few such players realize that NASA technology has been put to use in creating such games.

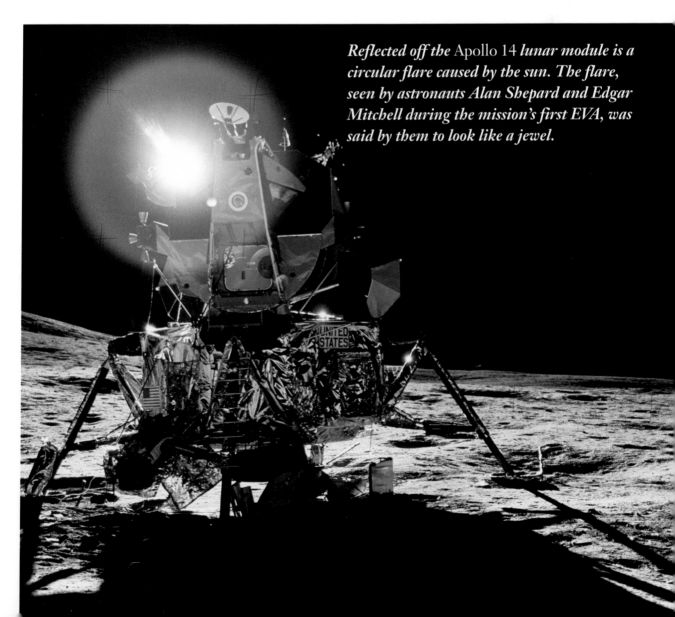

Reflected off the Apollo 14 **lunar module is a circular flare caused by the sun. The flare, seen by astronauts Alan Shepard and Edgar Mitchell during the mission's first EVA, was said by them to look like a jewel.**

Another type of EVA: Mission specialist Philippe Perrin works on installing systems for the Mobile Transporter, a railcar, on the International Space Station. Perrin is an astronaut for CNES, France's space agency.

Chapter Two

Space Stations

Do you play baseball? The helmet you wear at bat to protect your head may contain a foam padding that NASA first developed for astronauts' seats. Have you ever gone skiing? If you have, then the ski boots you wore are also a NASA spin-off. Ski boots are made so that skiers can flex their feet without losing any support. NASA first designed a flexible boot for astronauts to wear in space.

Baseball helmets and ski boots are just two of the many spinoffs from NASA that are now used in sports and recreation. Some of these spin-offs came from projects NASA developed to launch space stations into orbit around Earth. Space stations are places where astronauts live and work for long periods of time.

Space stations also give astronauts a good view of planets and other objects in space. Views of space from Earth are distorted by the **atmosphere**, layers of gases that surround the planet. These layers constantly shift and distort what we see of space from Earth. Being above the atmosphere gives astronauts a clearer view.

The Skylab 1 *space station orbits Earth in this photo taken by the Skylab 2 Command and Service Module during a routine "fly-around" inspection of the space station in June 1973.*

Skylab

The first American space station, called *Skylab*, was launched by NASA on May 14, 1973. NASA used parts salvaged from the Apollo project to build *Skylab*. The space station was 84 feet (26 m) long, weighed nearly 3 tons, and was the size of a three-bedroom house. In the first eight months after *Skylab*'s launch, NASA sent three crews of astronauts to live and work aboard the space station.

The main job of the first crew was to repair some damage that had occurred during liftoff. A shield had torn away. The shield was designed to protect *Skylab* from any meteoroid that might strike

Skylab *orbits Earth. At right on the vehicle is a solar panel. There was supposed to be a matching panel on* Skylab's *left side, but it was lost during deployment.*

it. A **meteoroid** is a small object made of rock or metal hurling through space.

The shield also served to block most of the Sun's rays to keep the temperature inside *Skylab* from getting too high. Without the shield, the temperature had risen to 126° F (52° C) inside *Skylab* when it was in the sun. On their second day in space, the astronauts fixed the problem. The crew spent twenty-eight days in space, breaking a Soviet record of twenty-three days set two years earlier. The Americans' record would not last long, however.

Space Record

The current world record for length of stay in space was set in 1994-1995 by a Russian astronaut who remained in space for 438 days.

Fellow member of the crew William R. Pogue took this photo of astronauts Jerry Carr, the mission commander (right), and Edward Gibson, the science pilot (left), at the far end of the orbital workshop aboard Skylab 4. *Also visible are three extra-vehicular mobility unit (EMU) space suits used for EVA.*

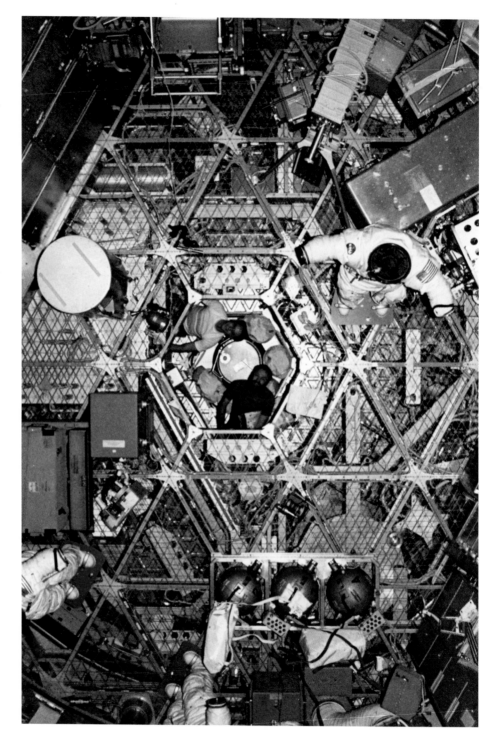

The next crew of astronauts sent to *Skylab* spent fifty-nine days in space. The third and final *Skylab* crew spent eighty-four days in space, traveling about 34 million miles (55 million km). Such long stays in space gave NASA the chance to study the effects of weightlessness on humans. An astronaut orbiting Earth is in a condition called **free fall**, the movement of an object toward Earth with little to slow the object down. While in free fall, astronauts can float inside their spacecraft. This makes them feel weightless. NASA discovered that astronauts did not experience any harmful effects from long periods of weightlessness.

NASA had hoped to keep *Skylab* in orbit until its next project was launched. To remain in orbit, *Skylab* would have to be boosted higher into space to keep it from falling back to Earth. But, NASA did not have the funds to do this. As a result, the space station fell back to Earth. On July 11, 1979, *Skylab* broke up as it reentered Earth's atmosphere and scattered in pieces over uninhabited regions of Australia and the Pacific Ocean. *Skylab* was not the only thing that had come to an end. By this time, the space competition between America and the Soviet Union had also ended.

Working Together

Besides sending astronauts to the Moon, Project Apollo was also used to establish a working relationship between the United States and the Soviet Union in space. In 1975, an Apollo spacecraft docked with a Soviet spacecraft while in

Growing Taller

Astronauts can grow 2 inches (5 centimeters) taller while in space because of weightlessness. Because an astronaut's spine does not have to support the body's weight in space, it can stretch slightly. After returning to Earth, the astronaut's spine shrinks to its original length as it again supports the body's weight.

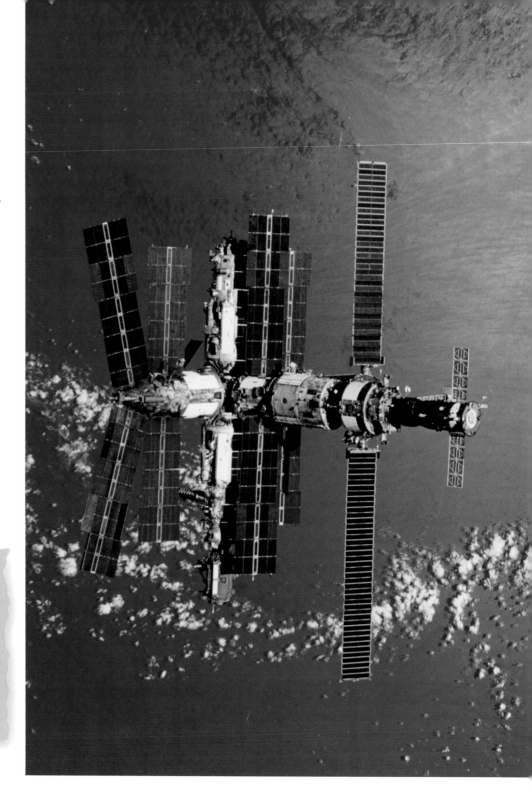

Taken from the space shuttle Atlantis, *this photograph shows Russia's space station,* Mir, *as* Atlantis *nears for docking in January 1997. The docking was to allow a U.S. astronaut aboard* Atlantis *to change places with a Russian cosmonaut aboard* Mir, *another of NASA's exercises in international cooperation in space.*

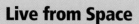

Live from Space

The first live telecast from space occurred in 1968 during the flight of *Apollo 7*, the first spacecraft to carry three American astronauts.

orbit. The astronauts were able to crawl from one spacecraft to another. When the two crews first met, they shook hands, an event that was televised live to Earth.

In 1986, the Soviet Union launched a space station called *Mir*. Seven American astronauts eventually lived aboard *Mir*, which remained in space until 1998. That same year, the first piece of the next and most ambitious space station was launched. This is the *International Space Station* (*ISS*).

Getting the *ISS* underway was no easy task. NASA originally budgeted $8 billion as its share of the cost of building the *ISS*. But this amount proved far too little. In the early 1990s, the *ISS* looked as if it would never get off the ground.

The unbearable lightness of being: Mission commander James Wetherbee, a U.S. astronaut, takes advantage of weightlessness to float about the Destiny *laboratory aboard the* International Space Station.

However, a deal between NASA and Russia was arranged. The first piece of the *ISS* was built and launched by Russia, but paid for by NASA. Today, sixteen nations are cooperating in building and operating the *ISS*.

The Biggest Thing in Orbit

Visible from Earth

The *ISS* can be seen from Earth. It looks like a bright star crossing the night sky.

Plans call for completing the *ISS* by early 2006. When finished, the *ISS* will be 290 feet (88 m) long and 360 feet (110 m) across. On Earth, the *ISS* would weigh nearly 500 tons. The size of two football fields placed side by side, the *ISS* will be the largest and heaviest object that humans have put into orbit around Earth.

The first crew boarded the *ISS* in November 2000. Like any new residents, the three astronauts—one American and two Russians—had to get used to their new living quarters. They had to wear earplugs to sleep because a machine that removed carbon dioxide from the air made a loud sound every ten minutes.

In 2001, NASA sent the Human Research Facility (HRF) to the *ISS*. The HRF was designed and built to measure changes in the astronauts' bodies during their long stays aboard the *ISS*. For example, the HRF will measure changes in an astronaut's ability to navigate. In this test, the astronaut wears a mask that is connected to a laptop computer. The mask allows the astronaut to see only what is on the computer screen. A program projects images of realistic tunnels through which the astronaut must navigate. The computer then analyzes the path the astronaut took to determine how well he or she navigated through the maze.

A Sports Spinoff

NASA has used the *ISS* to carry out experiments with various **memory metals**. These are metals that return to their original shape after they have been deliberately bent or twisted. NASA is experimenting with memory metals to find out if they are suitable for making airplane wings. Such wings would be flexible, allowing an airplane to perform maneuvers that are not possible now.

A memory metal developed by NASA is used to build the heads on some golf clubs. As the head strikes the golf ball, the metal changes shape. This change in shape keeps the club and ball in contact longer. As a result, the golf ball has more spin as it travels through the air. The extra spin causes the ball to stop more quickly when it hits the putting green. Many golfers may be able to improve their scores, thanks to this NASA spinoff. Another NASA project has led to even more spinoffs. This is the space shuttle.

Riding the back of a booster rocket, the space shuttle Endeavour *lifts off on June 5, 2002.* Endeavour's *destination on that mission was the* International Space Station. *Despite the* Challenger *and* Columbia *tragedies, the space shuttle is one of NASA's proudest achievements. It is the first craft capable of returning on its own to Earth.*

Chapter Three

The Space Shuttle

Like most young people, you probably like to play outdoors when the weather is nice. Unfortunately, some young people must be very careful whenever they go outdoors on a sunny day. These children suffer from a very rare medical condition—they do not have any sweat glands. Sweating is the body's way of keeping cool. Without sweat glands, these children can suffer heatstroke and even die by playing outdoors on a sunny day.

Those who have conducted EVA outside the space shuttle, like astronauts Linda Godwin (lower left) and Daniel Tani, seen here working on Endeavour, *report that it is one of the most exhilirating experiences imaginable.*

Fortunately, these children can now play outdoors whenever they want, thanks to NASA. All they have to do is wear a "cool suit." This suit is made of a special layer of clothing lined with plastic pouches that are filled with a waxy solid.

Outdoors, the waxy solid absorbs the heat from the Sun and slowly melts inside the pouches. By absorbing heat, the solid in the pouches keeps the child's body from overheating. The cool suit can be reused by placing the pouches in a refrigerator to turn the melted wax back into a solid. This cool suit is a spinoff of a space suit that NASA designed for astronauts to wear during their EVAs aboard the space shuttle.

A Reusable Spacecraft

Unlike the reusable cool suit, the spacecraft NASA launched in its Mercury, Gemini, and Apollo projects were good for only one use. Some of these spacecraft later made a trip to a museum. Not one, however, made another trip into space.

Building a new spacecraft for each launch cost a lot of money.

In the 1970s, NASA realized that future space missions would have to cost much less. One way to save money was to develop a spacecraft that could be reused as often as needed. In addition, NASA wanted to build a spacecraft that could deliver cargo into space. In this way, companies that wanted to launch their own satellites would help pay the cost of space missions. NASA's solution was to build the Space Transportation System, which is the space shuttle's official name. Although it is not completely reusable, the space shuttle has accomplished NASA's goal of saving money.

NASA launched the first shuttle, named *Columbia*, on April 12, 1981, from Cape Canaveral. Like all spacecraft launched by NASA, the shuttle travels into space aboard a rocket. But unlike earlier spacecraft, the shuttle returns from space like a plane.

The shuttle *Columbia* made five

NASA has so expanded the capabilities of space flight that repair missions, such as this March 2002 flight by the space shuttle Columbia *to provide maintenance on the* Hubble Space Telescope, *have come to seem almost routine. Astronauts James Newman and Michael Massimino can be seen here using* Columbia's *remote manipular arm to replace one of Hubble's cameras.*

successful trips in space. One goal of these missions was to test a robot arm. This device is used to remove cargo from the shuttle and place it in space. For its sixth shuttle mission, NASA launched its new shuttle named *Challenger*. Sally K. Ride became America's first woman astronaut on *Challenger's* second shuttle mission that was launched on June 18, 1983. The next *Challenger* flight, launched on August 30, 1983, brought another first: Guion S. Bluford became the first African-American in space.

The *Challenger* and *Columbia* Tragedies

Americans soon got used to a shuttle being launched into space on a regular basis. By the beginning of 1986, NASA had launched twenty-four successful shuttle missions. Then, on January 28, 1986, the second human tragedy in NASA's space program occurred. That morning, the shuttle *Challenger* again blasted off into space. Seven astronauts were aboard, including S. Christa McAuliffe, the first teacher to travel into space. Just seventy-three seconds after liftoff, *Challenger* blew up. All seven astronauts were killed.

NASA suspended future shuttle launches while it investigated the cause of the *Challenger* disaster. NASA discovered that a leaky seal allowed a booster rocket to break loose and drag *Challenger* out of control. Not until September 29, 1988, did NASA again launch a shuttle. After orbiting Earth for four days, *Discovery*, which had been redesigned, returned safely

The Space Shuttle

A space shuttle consists of three parts. One part is the orbiter, where the astronauts live and work. Two huge rocket boosters that lift the shuttle into orbit make up the second part. The third part is a large fuel tank that supplies the orbiter's three main engines. The fuel tank is the only part that is not reused. When all three parts are assembled and fueled, a space shuttle is about 184 feet (56 m) tall and weighs about 2,250 tons.

home. NASA was back in business with the space shuttle. However, another tragedy struck the space shuttle program on February 1, 2003.

On the way home after a sixteen-day mission, the space shuttle *Columbia* broke apart shortly after reentering Earth's atmosphere. The shuttle was traveling at about 12,500 miles (20,000 km) per hour some 38 miles (61 km) above land when the tragedy occurred. Investigators discovered that super-heated gases may have penetrated the space shuttle through damaged surface tiles on its left wing. These gases then caused

Columbia to break apart. The seven astronauts aboard, including six Americans and the first Israeli in space, were killed.

Eye in the Sky

When the shuttle *Discovery* took off in April 1990, attention was focused not on the astronauts, but on the cargo that was aboard. The shuttle was carrying the *Hubble Space Telescope* (*HST*). The astronauts aboard used the shuttle's robot arm to remove the *HST* from the cargo bay and place it in orbit about 370 miles (595 km) above Earth. Equipped with cutting-edge technology, the *HST* was designed to take a close look into deep space.

The *HST* has provided the closest and clearest look at distant planets, such as Uranus, Neptune, and Pluto. The *HST* has also taken images of galaxies so far away that it has in effect looked back some 11 billion years, at a time when the universe was young. But the images that the *HST* is now providing were not always clear. When it was first put into orbit in 1990, the *HST* could not focus properly. In 1993, NASA launched its sixty-first shuttle mission. The main job of the astronauts aboard was to fix the problem with the *HST*.

Since that successful repair, NASA has launched three more shuttle missions to update the *HST*. The latest was the shuttle *Columbia*, launched on March 1, 2002. During their EVAs, the astronauts installed some 6,000 pounds (2,700 kg) of equipment on the *HST*. One item was a camera that is about the size of a telephone booth.

Shuttle Service

The last shuttle to service the *HST* is scheduled for launch in 2004. This should enable the space telescope to complete its twenty-year mission in 2010.

The great canyon known as Valle Marineris is clearly visible as it cuts across the surface of Mars in this NASA image. The dark, reddish spots near the top of the planet are the three giant volcanoes of Tharsis.

Chapter Four

Exploring Distant Planets

Have you ever had your temperature taken by a thermometer that was put in your ear? The thermometer detects heat given off by the eardrum. A tiny computer chip converts this heat to a temperature that is displayed digitally. Some ear thermometers do this in two seconds or less. The ear thermometer is a spinoff of a device NASA installed on its spacecraft to measure the temperature of distant planets.

NASA's First Launch

The first NASA project designed to explore the solar system beyond Earth was called Pioneer. The first satellite ever launched by NASA was appropriately called *Pioneer 1*. The launch took place on October 11, 1958, less than three months after NASA had been established. NASA planned to send *Pioneer 1* into orbit around the Moon. But, the satellite traveled only about 70,789 miles (113,854 km), or about one-quarter of the distance to the Moon.

NASA launched a total of thirteen Pioneer satellites over a period of twenty years. Launched in 1972, *Pioneer 10* flew by Jupiter and then became the first human-made object ever to leave our solar system. In 1979, *Pioneer 11* flew within 13,000 miles (20,900 km) of Saturn.

In the late 1970s, *Pioneer 12* and *Pioneer 13* orbited Venus and mapped the planet's surface. *Pioneer 13* also sent four probes through the Venusian atmosphere. One landed on the surface of Venus and sent signals back to Earth for more than an hour before its batteries drained. With the success of its Pioneer project, NASA had probed into the far reaches of space. But it was just the beginning of what NASA would find out about the solar system.

Studying the Solar System

The list of spacecraft that NASA has launched to study the solar system is long. Since *Pioneer 4* became NASA's first spacecraft to travel outside Earth's orbit on its way to the

First in Space

The United States launched its first satellite, *Explorer 1*, into orbit around Earth on January 31, 1958. The Soviet Union had launched a satellite called *Sputnik 1* into orbit almost four months earlier.

Moon in 1959, spacecraft have orbited or flown by all the planets except Pluto. The information that these spacecraft have collected has filled many books. What follows are only a few of the many interesting discoveries that NASA spacecraft have made about our solar system, starting with the Sun.

The spacecraft *SOHO* detected steady wind speeds on the Sun that reach 198,800 miles per hour (320,000 km per hour). At this speed, winds would take less than a minute to cross the Atlantic Ocean.

Mercury has been visited by only one spacecraft, *Mariner 10*, which found an extreme range of temperatures on the planet. Mercury has almost the highest temperatures of any planet in the solar system and almost the coldest temperatures.

Venus is surrounded by dense clouds that made it impossible to see its surface until the spacecraft *Magellan* arrived.

Visiting Pluto

NASA hopes to launch a spacecraft in early 2006 that will arrive at Pluto some time between 2015 and 2017.

Mariner 10 provided this image of the surface of the planet Mercury. Scientists speculate that the light blue areas in the image may be ancient volcanoes.

This computer-generated representation of the surface of the planet Venus is based on data collected by Magellan. *The image shows three craters—Howe, Danilova, and Aglaonice—in the northwest region of Lavinia Planitia in Venus's southern hemisphere.*

Using radar, *Magellan* mapped more than 98 percent of the planet's surface and revealed that it is covered with volcanic material, such as lava.

Mars became the first planet after Earth to have a human-made object orbit it. While orbiting Mars, *Mariner 9* discovered the largest known volcano in the solar system. Named Olympus Mons, this volcano is 17 miles (27 km) high and 373 miles (600 km) wide.

The spacecraft *Galileo* dropped a probe into Jupiter's atmosphere, which sent back important information about its composition.

Saturn has been visited by two *Voyager* spacecraft. The planet is surrounded by an enormous system of rings. These rings are so large that they would extend from the Earth to the Moon. The *Voyager* spacecraft discovered that Saturn's rings are made mostly of ice.

When *Voyager 2* visited Uranus, it discovered ten more moons orbiting the planet. Uranus is now known to have twenty-one moons.

Neptune was also photographed by *Voyager 2*. The spacecraft discovered six new moons and three new rings that orbit the planet.

This color-enhanced view of Mars shows dark patches on the planet's surface. The image was sent back to Earth by the Mars Global Surveyor.

Back on Earth

The technologies that NASA developed to explore our solar system have led to spinoffs now used for health care. Ear thermometers are just one example. Another such spinoff is a vision screening system for children. A digital camera takes images of a child's eyes. In less than one minute, a computer analyzes the images for various vision problems. During the early 1990s, about 50,000 American children were screened using this system. About 4,000 were given immediate medical attention to prevent them from developing permanent vision problems.

Straight Teeth

Clear braces that are almost invisible are another NASA spinoff.

Although NASA's mission is space, much of its work has applications back here on Earth. This photo, taken from the space shuttle Atlantis *in January 1997, shows the delta of the Nile River, in Egypt, with the huge city of Cairo on the east (right) bank.*

Chapter Five

Planet Earth

People use many NASA spinoffs in their daily lives. These spinoffs are considered *indirect* benefits of NASA's work because they are based on technologies that NASA first developed for their space program. For example, NASA developed rechargeable, long-life batteries to power the instruments on spacecraft. These batteries led to the rechargeable batteries that are used to power devices that we use every day.

But people have also benefited *directly* from NASA programs. For example, weather satellites provide continuous information about our global climate.

Their warnings about approaching storms, such as the hurricane that struck Florida in 1992, have saved many lives. These satellites have also warned us of an even more serious threat to planet Earth.

The Ozone Layer

In the 1980s, a weather satellite, *Nimbus* 7, confirmed that a problem had developed with the ozone layer. **Ozone** is a chemical produced when sunlight strikes oxygen in the air. Ozone forms a thin layer that surrounds Earth about 12 to 30 miles (19 to 48 km) above sea level.

The ozone layer blocks most of the Sun's ultraviolet light from reaching Earth. If more ultraviolet light did reach Earth, it would damage plant and animal life and cause a large increase in the number of people with skin cancer. Images provided by *Nimbus* 7 showed that a huge hole had formed in the ozone layer. This hole, which appears over Antarctica for several months every year, is growing bigger. In 2000, the hole measured about 11 million square miles (28 million square km), larger than the entire North American continent.

Scientists concluded that the hole was caused by chemicals used in aerosol sprays, refrigerators, and air-conditioning systems. These chemicals slowly drift to the upper atmosphere where they break apart the ozone. The images provided by NASA weather satellites helped convince countries to ban the use of these chemicals. Scientists hope that the ozone layer will be able to repair itself.

Rather Thin

The ozone layer is only the thickness of two stacked pennies.

44

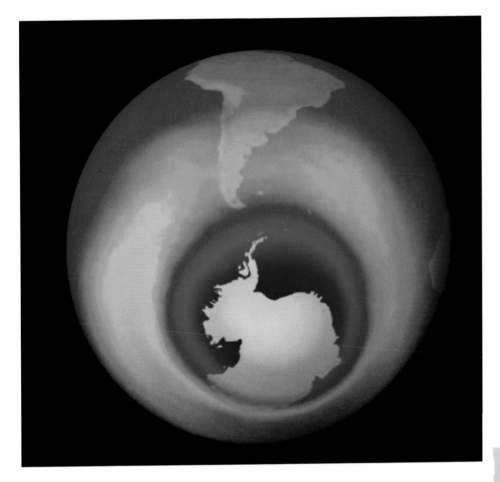

NASA's TOMS (Total Ozone Mapping Spectrometer) Earth Probe shows clearly, in blue, the depletion of the ozone layer over Antarctica. Damage to the ozone layer is a primary cause of global warming.

View from Space

The process of taking close-up images of Earth from space is called remote sensing.

Watching over Earth

Partly because of what *Nimbus 7* had discovered, NASA began a program in 1991 to study Earth much more closely than it had. NASA calls its new program Earth Science Enterprise. For this program, spacecraft were not launched to some distant part of the solar system, but rather sent into orbit around Earth.

Cameras and other instruments onboard spacecraft in orbit provide close-up images and other information about our

Taken with a handheld camera through a window of the space shuttle Atlantis, *this photograph shows the great commercial city-state of Singapore, on the Malay peninsula in southeast Asia. Images such as this one can be used to study the effects of urbanization on the land and environment over time.*

NASA and Farming

NASA uses cameras to photograph farmers' fields. These cameras photograph not only what the human eye *can* see but also what it *cannot* see. Images are taken of a field as it appears in visible light, which we can see, and also in infrared light, which we cannot see.

Healthy plants reflect infrared light well. But plants that are wilted or infected with insects do not reflect infrared light as well. As a result, plants that need attention appear darker in images taken with infrared light.

These images are sent to the farmer in as little as twenty-four hours. A farmer can then attend to the problem before any serious damage is done.

planet's land, water, and air. These images and information are used in making plans to control damage from disasters, such as wildfires and floods, and to manage resources, such as forests and farmlands.

To see how NASA helps farmers plan, consider Neal Isbell whose family has been growing crops in northern Alabama for six generations. Isbell is one of a new generation of farmers who practice "precision agriculture." These farmers use information provided by NASA satellites and planes to determine which areas in their fields need fertilizer, water, or weed control. As a result, these farmers do not have to waste time

One practical application on Earth of NASA observation technology is in the field known as precision agriculture. Data collected by the ATLAS remote sensing instrument aboard a NASA airplane is used to create an image, such as this one, of a particular plot of land. Trained observers can use the image to obtain information about such things as the content and health of soil, availability of water, evaporation, and overall suitability for agriculture.

tending to crops that do not require care. These farmers also save money, especially by not using fertilizers where they are not needed. With 4,200 acres (1,700 hectares) of cotton to care for, Isbell has saved a lot of time and money.

Uncovering the Past

Images taken by NASA satellites and planes have also uncovered information about Earth's past. In 1981, images from a space shuttle discovered the lost city of Ubar in the Sahara Desert in Africa. Instruments aboard the shuttle recorded images of a network of tracks that helped pinpoint the city, which lay buried beneath the desert sand. NASA

NASA imaging technology can even be used to gain knowledge about human history. This radar image obtained by the space shuttle Endeavour *in April 1994 was used to determine the location of the lost city of Ubar, a remote desert trading outpost in what is now the nation of Oman on the Arabian peninsula. Ubar vanished from recorded history in about the year 300, but this image revealed ancient tracks (thin reddish streaks near center) leading to and from the lost trade center.*

images also revealed that the Sahara, the driest place on Earth, once had rivers and lakes.

Images taken from a shuttle also revealed a hidden section of the ancient city of Angkor in Cambodia. During the ninth century, the city was home to more than one million people. Today, much of it is covered by a thick jungle. NASA images detected canals north of the main city that cannot be seen from the ground. Scientists now believe that Angkor was even larger than they had once thought.

Extraterrestrial Life

In 2002, NASA asked about 100 scientists to meet and discuss one issue: Does extraterrestrial life exist? In other words, does life exist someplace in the universe other than Earth? This is an appropriate question for NASA to explore. After all, NASA has launched dozens of missions to study our solar system and to peer into the far reaches of our universe. NASA has also launched spacecraft to take a close look at Earth, including its life-forms. So it's logical for NASA to explore whether life, which is found everywhere on Earth, exists anywhere else in our universe.

The search for extraterrestrial life has led to a new branch of science called **astrobiology**, which is the study of the origin, evolution, and distribution of life in the universe. To find life as we know it elsewhere in the universe, scientists must first find an Earth-like planet. Earth is a **terrestrial planet**, one made of solid materials like rocks and metals. In addition

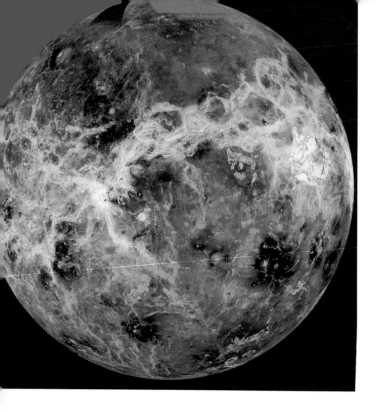

Data provided by Venera 13 *and* 14, Magellan, *and* Pioneer *was used to create this image of Venus, showing the topography of the planet.*

to Earth, the terrestrial planets in our solar system are Mercury, Venus, Mars, and Pluto. Jupiter, Saturn, Neptune, and Uranus are known as **gas giants**, because they are huge balls of gases and liquids.

Telescopes on Earth have so far found more than a hundred planets orbiting nearby stars. However, all of these planets are gas giants, where life is not likely to exist. Over the next two decades, NASA will launch several missions to search a part of the Milky Way galaxy for terrestrial planets. One, called the *Kepler* mission, is scheduled for launch in 2007. The satellite, which will be placed into orbit around the Sun, will study 100,000 other distant stars, looking for terrestrial planets.

Finding a terrestrial planet orbiting a distant star is no easy task. The planet must pass in front of the star as seen from Earth and block enough of the star's light for scientists to determine if it is a terrestrial planet. NASA scientists have compared what they must do to the challenge of finding an ant crawling across the headlight of one car miles away on a highway filled with cars, all with their headlights on. This challenge may seem impossible. However, the challenge of sending astronauts to the Moon also seemed impossible at one time. NASA proved it could be done.

Astronaut Alan Shepard plants the U.S. flag on the Moon. Putting a man on the moon is one of NASA's greatest accomplishments; it is a feat that no other country has come close to duplicating.

NASA—A Timeline

1957	The Soviet Union launches the first artificial satellite, *Sputnik 1*.
1958	The United States launches its first satellite, *Explorer 1*. (January) The law establishing NASA is signed. (July) NASA launches *Pioneer 1*. (October)
1959	NASA launches *Pioneer 4* to the Moon. (March) NASA selects its first seven astronauts, known as the Mercury 7. (April)
1960	NASA launches the first weather satellite, *TIROS 1*, and the first communications satellite, *Echo 1*.
1961	Alan Shepard becomes America's first astronaut in space.
1962	John Glenn becomes the first American to orbit Earth.
1965	NASA launches its first manned Gemini mission. (March) Edward White becomes the first American to walk in space. (June)
1966	NASA lands an unmanned spacecraft on the Moon.
1967	Three astronauts are killed in a fire while performing a ground test of an Apollo spacecraft.
1968	NASA launches its first successful manned Apollo mission.
1969	Two Apollo astronauts, Neil Armstrong and Edwin Aldrin, walk on the Moon.
1972	The last Apollo mission returns from the Moon.
1973	NASA launches *Skylab*. (May) NASA sends its first unmanned mission to fly by two planets, Venus and Mercury. (November)
1977	*Voyager 1* and *Voyager 2* are launched to study the giant gas planets.

1981	NASA launches its first space shuttle.
1983	Sally K. Ride becomes the first American woman in space. Guion S. Bluford becomes the first African American in space.
1986	Seven astronauts are killed when the shuttle *Challenger* explodes shortly after launch.
1990	The *Hubble Space Telescope* is placed in orbit around Earth.
1998	NASA begins construction of the *International Space Station*, which is scheduled for completion in 2006.
2002	NASA gathers scientists to plan missions to look for extraterrestrial life.
2003	Seven astronauts are killed when the space shuttle *Columbia* breaks apart while returning to Earth.

Glossary

astrobiology—the study of the origin, evolution, and distribution of life in the universe

atmosphere—the layers of gases that surround a planet

extra-vehicular activity (EVA)—an activity performed in space by an astronaut outside a spacecraft; commonly referred to as a space walk

free fall—the movement of an object toward Earth with little to slow it down

gas giant—a planet such as Jupiter that is a huge ball of gases and liquids

memory metal—a metal that returns to its original shape after it has been deliberately bent or twisted

meteoroid—a small object made of rock or metal hurling through space

orbit—to travel around a particular object in space; the path an object takes as it travels around another object in space

ozone—a chemical that forms a layer above Earth that protects against the Sun's ultraviolet light

satellite—any object that orbits another object in space. Earth is a natural satellite of the Sun. The *Hubble Space Telescope* is an artificial satellite, or one made by humans, of Earth.

Soviet Union—a nation formed in 1922 when Russia combined with other countries in eastern Europe and central Asia. It broke apart in 1991.

spinoff—an object or device that was originally designed for some other use

terrestrial planet—a planet such as Earth that is made of solid materials like rocks and metals

To Find Out More

Books

Baker, David. Scientific American *Inventions from Outer Space: Everyday Uses for NASA Technology*. New York: Random House, 2000.

Bredeson, Carmen. *NASA Planetary Spacecraft*. Berkeley Heights, NJ: Enslow, 2000.

Campbell, Ann-Jeanette. *The New York Public Library's Amazing Space: A Book of Answers for Kids*. New York: Wiley, 1997.

Cole, Michael D. *NASA Space Vehicles*. Berkeley Heights, NJ: Enslow, 2000.

Jones, Thomas D., and Michael Benson. *The Complete Idiot's Guide to NASA*. Indianapolis, IN: Alpha Books, 2002.

Mullane, R. Mike. *Do Your Ears Pop in Space?: And 500 Surprising Questions about Space Travel*. New York: Wiley, 1997.

Spangenburg, Ray, and Kit Moser. *The History of NASA*. Danbury, CT: Franklin Watts, 2000.

Organizations and Online Sites

NASA Space Camp

http://www.spacecamp.com/spacecamp/

Find out how you can train like an astronaut. NASA operates two Space Camps in the United States for kids ages nine and older. This site has information about the program, including the dates and prices.

NASA Visitors Center and Tours

http://www.nasa.gov/about/visiting/

You can get information about the National Air and Space Museum in Washington, D.C., where you can see a collection of spacecraft used in NASA missions. This site also lists NASA centers located throughout the United States where visitors are welcome. One such center is the Kennedy Space Center in Cape Canaveral, Florida, where you can see a space shuttle launch.

National Aeronautics and Space Administration
Headquarters Information Center
Washington, D.C. 20546-0001
http://www.hq.nasa.gov/office/hqlibrary/ic/nasaic.htm
info-center@hq.nasa.gov
The NASA Information Center provides information brochures, mission decals, and posters for free and also sells various publications.

National Aeronautics and Space Administration
http://www.nasa.gov
The NASA home page includes NASA for Kids, Webcasts that are available for downloading, and updated information about the *International Space Station.*

National Space Society
600 Pennsylvania Avenue, S.E.
Suite 201
Washington, D.C. 20003
http://www.nss.org
Click on "Education" to get information about *The Space Educator,* a free publication.

A Note on Sources

My first step in writing this book was to get an overall view of what NASA has done since it started operating in 1958. I quickly learned that plenty of information exists. Many books have been written about each project that NASA has undertaken. Trying to sort through all this information would have taken a long time.

I soon realized that I needed to find a source that provided an overview of what NASA has done. In this way, I could select certain missions to focus on and then search other sources for additional details. Because there are so many names, dates, and places involved, I also wanted to be sure that my basic source was up-to-date and reliable. Ideally, it would be written by someone who could provide a first-hand account of some of NASA's projects and have direct access to information about its other projects. *The Complete Idiot's Guide to NASA*, which was written by former astronaut Thomas D. Jones and

Michael Benson, became the starting point for each chapter in this book. Dr. Jones has flown on three of the four space shuttles in operation today.

Another up-to-date and reliable source of information was NASA itself. Finding the right people at NASA, sending them my questions, and then waiting for their responses would be time-consuming. So I decided to check out NASA on the Internet. Using a search engine, I typed in certain keywords. For example, the keywords "NASA" and "astrobiology" gave me the information I used to write about the space agency's mission to search for extraterrestrial life. The keywords "NASA" and "spinoffs" led me to all sorts of everyday devices that were developed by the space agency. I owe a special thanks to NASA for posting so much information about their missions on the Internet.

Index

Numbers in *italics* indicate illustrations.

About the Author

Salvatore Tocci taught high school and college science for almost thirty years. He has a bachelor's degree from Cornell University and a master's degree from the City University of New York.

He has written books that deal with a range of science topics, from biographies of famous scientists to a high school chemistry text. He has also presented workshops at national science conventions showing teachers how to emphasize the applications of scientific knowledge in our everyday lives.

Tocci lives in East Hampton, New York, with his wife, Patti. Both retired from teaching, they spend their leisure time sailing and traveling. On a recent trip to Florida, they went to Cape Canaveral to see a shuttle launch. Unfortunately, it was postponed.